W9-BZX-799

BUCK
LEONARD

Simone Payment

Published in 2002 by The Rosen Publishing Group, Inc.
29 East 21st Street, New York, NY 10010

First Edition

Library of Congress Cataloging-in-Publication Data

Payment, Simone.
Buck Leonard / Simone Payment.— 1st ed.
p. cm. — (Baseball Hall of Famers of the Negro Leagues)
Includes bibliographical references and index.
ISBN 0-8239-3473-X (lib. bdg.)
1. Leonard, Buck, 1907– 2. Baseball players—United States—
Biography. 3. Afro-American baseball players—Biography. 4. Negro
leagues—History. I. Title. II. Series.
GV865.L45 P39 2002
796.357'092—dc21

2001003151

Manufactured in the United States of America

Contents

During the first half of the twentieth century, African American children in North Carolina, where Buck Leonard grew up, were not permitted to attend school—or even to play baseball—with white children.

Introduction

I magine you are a boy who loves baseball. You are seven years old and you sometimes play baseball using a broom handle for a bat and a rock for a ball. One day you go to a park near your house to see a team play a baseball game with a real bat and a real ball. You are not allowed to enter the baseball park, so you and some others watch through the fence. Suddenly, along comes a policeman who arrests you and takes you to jail—all because your skin is black, and the skin of the baseball players on the team and the policeman who arrested you is white.

Buck Leonard was that little boy. He never dreamed that he would be a star player in the

Negro leagues when he grew up. And he never imagined that one day he would join the greatest baseball players of all time in the Baseball Hall of Fame. But Buck Leonard grew up to be one of the best first basemen and best hitters in the history of baseball.

You might not know as much about Buck Leonard as you know about white baseball players like Babe Ruth or Lou Gehrig, who played baseball when Leonard was young. Leonard grew up in a time when African Americans could not play on major league baseball teams. Because African Americans were not considered equal with white people and had to go to separate schools, churches, and restaurants, they formed their own teams and organized their own leagues—the Negro leagues—so that they could play baseball.

Life for Leonard and other players in the Negro leagues was not always easy. They did not make as much money as did the white major leaguers. They were not allowed to stay in the same hotels as white players or eat at the same

A group of African American athletes meet for a Negro league baseball game in Atlanta, Georgia, in early 1939.

restaurants. According to Leonard, as an African American baseball player, one "always had to remember that you were black [and] there were certain places you couldn't go and things you couldn't do." But Leonard and his teammates in the Negro leagues were doing what they wanted to do: They were playing baseball. Leonard says they loved it and just played "for the fun of it."

From the time the Negro leagues were organized, in 1920, they were an important part of life for many African Americans. The leagues gave players a chance to travel the country playing baseball and to be paid for it. They gave African American baseball fans games to look forward to and players to admire.

Jackie Robinson, shown here playing second base for the Brooklyn Dodgers, broke baseball's color barrier when he joined the major leagues in 1945.

In 1945, things changed for the Negro leagues. That's when a man named Jackie Robinson became the first African American to agree to join a white major league baseball team. That began the process of integration, and other Negro leaguers began to join major league teams. This was an exciting time for fans and players. Finally, African American players were given the chance to succeed in the major leagues. Fans followed their favorite Negro league players on their new major league teams. But integration changed the Negro leagues. Soon, there were few good men left playing on the Negro league teams. By the time integration started, Buck Leonard and some of the other stars of the Negro leagues were too old to join a major league team, but they continued to play baseball because they loved the game and were not ready to give it up. Leonard regrets that he never had a chance to play in the major leagues, but he says that he would not change the way things were. He would do it all again, as long as he could play baseball.

Buck Leonard did not play on a professional Negro league baseball team until he was twenty-five years old. He had played for local teams in his hometown of Rocky Mount, North Carolina, and had played for a few semiprofessional teams. But in 1934, he got his chance to play in the Negro leagues for the Homestead Grays. For the next seventeen years, he played for the Grays, becoming their star first baseman and an excellent hitter. Leonard was the Negro National League batting champion in 1937, 1938, and 1948 and hit as high as .500. His superior hitting helped make the Grays a powerful team. They won nine pennants in a row from 1937 to 1945.

Besides being a great baseball player, Buck Leonard was also the kind of man people instantly liked. He was respected by all of his teammates, and he was always willing to offer advice to young players. Leonard always worked very hard to improve his playing. Even if it seemed clear that his team was going to

win a game, Leonard still played hard. And
although he was a very successful player, he
never let that go to his head. He was a talented
athlete and a great human being.

Buck Leonard got his big professional break when he joined the
Homestead Grays in 1934. His stellar record with the Grays would
eventually pave the way for him to be inducted into the Baseball
Hall of Fame.

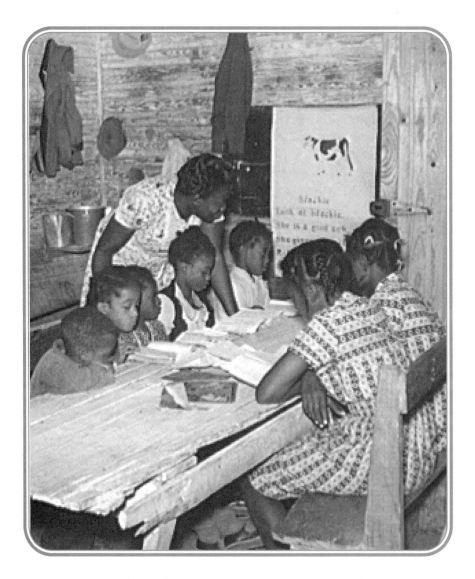

This 1939 photo of a school in Mississippi shows the inferior conditions of segregated schools for African American children throughout the South.

Before the Negro Leagues

Walter Fenner "Buck" Leonard was born in Rocky Mount, North Carolina, on September 8, 1907. His father, John, was a railroad fireman. His mother, Emma, stayed at home to take care of Buck and his three sisters and two brothers. The Leonard family lived in a neighborhood called Little Raleigh, where they raised chickens, ducks, geese, and hogs.

When Buck Leonard was young, his parents called him Buddy. But his little brother Charlie could not say Buddy and instead called him Bucky. That name stuck, and when he got older, his nickname was shortened to Buck.

When Buck was six, he started school at the Lincoln Elementary School. On his first day, the teacher made him write with his right hand, even though he was more comfortable using his left. When he began playing baseball, he batted and threw the ball with his left hand.

First Interest in Baseball

Rocky Mount had a white baseball team that played at a ballpark near Buck Leonard's home. When he was about seven years old, Leonard would go to the park and peek through the cracks in the fence to watch the game. At that time, America was segregated. In 1896, the Supreme Court had decided a case called *Plessy v. Ferguson,* which ruled that it was legal in the United States to have "separate but equal" restaurants, bathrooms, schools—even water fountains—for African Americans and whites. A Montgomery, Alabama, law stated that a white man and an African American man could not play checkers together in a public place.

This sign at a Greyhound bus station in 1943 was a familiar sight during segregation. Signs reading "Whites only" were also widely used.

Baseball was no exception. There were white baseball teams and white baseball parks. African Americans had their own teams and sometimes their own baseball parks, and they were not allowed in the white baseball parks. Looking through the fence was as close as young Buck Leonard could get. One night the police came and arrested Leonard and everyone else watching the game through the fence.

When they were taken to court, the judge told them that they had to stand five feet away from the fence. The next time they went to a game, Leonard and his friends brought boxes to stand on so they could see over the fence. But the police wouldn't allow that either.

About a year later, Rocky Mount built an African American baseball park, and an African American baseball team began playing there. The team played other teams from nearby

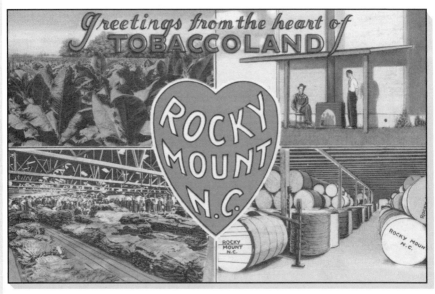

As suggested by this postcard, tobacco was one of the main industries in Rocky Mount, North Carolina, Buck Leonard's hometown.

towns. Leonard went to every game and became a batboy for the team. He picked up the bats and helped the players, and he learned about playing baseball.

Leonard joined the baseball team at his school when he was about ten. He wanted to play football, but his mother wouldn't let him. She didn't like him playing baseball either, but she allowed it. Leonard was one of the youngest players and could not travel with the team until he was twelve years old. At one of the first games he was allowed to travel to, he had to crawl under a building to get a ball that had gotten past him while he was playing center field. His belt got stuck on a nail, trapping him under the building. At that same game, he struck out and cried. It was a rough start!

Going to Work

In 1919, when Leonard was eleven years old, his father died. Leonard's oldest sister quit school and went to work to help support the family. Because Leonard was the oldest boy, he had to help out, too. After school each day he worked in a sock factory. Two years later, the factory closed, so Leonard took a job shining shoes at the local railroad station.

At that time, there were no high schools for African American students. If they wanted to continue their education, they went to an African American college. Because Leonard had to help support his family, he could not go to college. He finished the eighth grade and continued to shine shoes at the railroad station for about two more years. When he was sixteen, he got a job at the Atlantic Coastline Railroad Shop and worked there for the next nine years. His first job was picking up trash in the train yard. He did that for a year and made about $1.80 a day. After that he got a job working in the office at the railroad.

During the time that Leonard was working for the railroad, he got a chance to go to Washington, D.C., to see the New York Yankees play. It was the Fourth of July, and Leonard was seventeen years old. He made the trip alone and was very excited to see Lou Gehrig, the Yankees' famous first baseman. Gehrig was his favorite player, and Leonard tried to bat and field just like him. He must have done a good job studying Gehrig because when Leonard began playing baseball professionally, he was often called the Black Lou Gehrig.

The Rocky Mount Black Swans

While Leonard was working for the railroad, he spent many of his evenings and weekends playing baseball for his hometown teams. The teams were called the Rocky Mount Black Swans and the Rocky Mount Elks, and they played against other local African American teams. Leonard would get out of work at 3:30 and would quickly ride his bike to the baseball field. He would change his clothes just in time to start the game at 4:00. Because the fields where they played had no lights, they could not play games past sundown.

Leonard's brother Charlie also played on the Swans and was sometimes the pitcher. Buck tried pitching but wasn't very good at it, so he played center field. When he was seventeen, he also began managing the team. Part of his job as a manager was to argue calls made by the umpire. One night, the regular first baseman on the team could not make it, so Leonard played first base. When he played first base, he was closer to the umpire, which made it easier to

Buck Leonard worked assorted railroad jobs while playing for his hometown teams.

argue with him. Leonard soon decided that he would become the regular first baseman. He played first base for the rest of his career.

The Black Swans did not get paid a regular salary. If there was money left over after the team paid the expenses—such as renting the field, buying balls, and paying umpires—the players would divide it. Each player might get two or three dollars for each game.

During the day, Leonard was still working for the railroad. After about a year in the office, he got a job putting brakes on and cleaning the boxcars. His pay was better, but he still did not make much money. Leonard could not belong to a union because he was African American. Even though his pay was not always fair, Leonard worked in the train yard for the next seven years. Then the Depression hit, and many people in America lost their jobs and all of their money. Leonard had to give up his job to a white man and take a lower-paying one. About a year later, he lost that job and began working part-time at a funeral home. At the funeral home,

Leonard met Sarah Wroten, the woman who would later become his wife. The funeral home job didn't last long: Buck Leonard soon got an exciting offer to earn money playing baseball.

Dougherty's Black Revels

Leonard might have continued to play baseball just for fun if he had not been laid off by the railroad. Jobs were scarce, and even though he worked part-time at the funeral home, Leonard was not making enough money to live on. His luck changed when a semiprofessional team called Dougherty's Black Revels offered him fifteen dollars a week to play. The team played in Portsmouth, North Carolina, and it was Leonard's first time living away from home. He was a little homesick, but he played very well there and got along with the people in the town. One of his best games was against a team from Rocky Mount. In that game, Leonard hit a triple, stole four bases, had four RBIs (runs batted in), and he got a hit all four times he was at bat. His new team won 9–0.

A Brief History of the Negro Leagues

In the 1800s, when baseball was in its infancy in America, some African Americans played on the same teams as whites. Those players faced prejudice on the field and off, and soon it became clear that African Americans would not be accepted on the same teams as whites. There were no laws that stated this, but it was understood. As a result, African Americans began forming their own teams and traveling the country playing games wherever they could. It wasn't until 1920 that Rube Foster—known as the father of black baseball—organized eight of the teams to form the Negro National League. Times were tough for the teams in the league. They had trouble finding parks where they could play, and it was always hard to earn enough money. Although that league was forced to fold because of financial reasons, a new Negro National League was formed in 1933. Other leagues were formed, but most did not last long. Another strong league was formed in 1937. That league, called the Negro American League, included teams from the South and the West. Both leagues continued until African American players were finally allowed to join the major leagues.

The Baltimore Stars

About three months after Leonard joined the Black Revels, they played another team, called the Baltimore Stars. Ben Taylor, the manager of the Stars, saw Leonard play and offered him a job with the team. He told Leonard that he could make more money playing for the Stars. Also, Leonard's brother Charlie played for the team, so Leonard decided he would join, too. He didn't receive a salary with the Stars; he just got part of what the team earned each night. Many people told him it would be difficult to earn enough money to live on, but Leonard decided to try it anyway.

At first it was difficult. The Stars earned $20 to $30 a night, and that had to be shared by each member of the team. Leonard learned a lot while playing for the Stars, however. His manager had been a great first baseman, and he taught Leonard many things about playing that position.

The Stars were having a hard time finding enough games around Baltimore, so Ben Taylor

Buck Leonard reaches to make a play during a Negro league game.

decided to move the team to New York City. The players lived in a hotel, ten men to a room. Unfortunately, there weren't enough games in New York either, and finally the Stars were forced to break up. Because they didn't have enough money to check out of the hotel, they sold the team's cars to pay the bill. Then Buck and Charlie Leonard were stuck in New York City with no money, no jobs, and no way to get home.

The Brooklyn Royal Giants

Buck Leonard was able to get Charlie a ride home to Rocky Mount so Charlie could go back to college. But Leonard knew he would have to find another baseball job. Luckily, he met Dick Redding, who was the manager of the Brooklyn Royal Giants. Even though Dick Redding had never seen Leonard play, he agreed to hire him. Leonard started the next day.

The Brooklyn Royal Giants were more skilled than the Baltimore Stars. They played other teams around New York. Sometimes, the team would travel to towns in New York State and play games at county fairs. They would play in city parks, fairgrounds, or any empty stretch of land they could find.

At the end of the baseball season, Leonard wasn't sure what to do. He received an offer to play on a team in Puerto Rico, but the offer fell through. So he took what little money he had left and bought a bus ticket home to Rocky Mount. He was glad to go home.

The next spring, Leonard went back to Brooklyn to start another season with the Royal Giants. One day while he was practicing with the team, Smokey Joe Williams saw him play. Smokey Joe had played with the Homestead Grays, a Negro league team, but was retired at that time. He thought that Leonard was good enough to play for the Grays. Leonard wasn't sure he wanted to go to Pittsburgh, Pennsylvania, where the Grays were based, but he agreed to talk to the owner of the team. When Cumberland "Cum" Posey, the owner of the team, offered him $125 a month to play with the Grays, Leonard jumped at the chance. He was about to start his adventure in the Negro leagues.

This landscape photo of Homestead, Pennsylvania, (circa 1900)
shows the steelworks and smokestacks of the industrial town.

The Negro Leagues: Life on the Field

The day after Buck Leonard got a job playing for the Homestead Grays, he boarded a bus at midnight. The bus drove through the night and arrived in Wheeling, West Virginia, the next day. Wheeling was where the Homestead Grays were having spring training. When Cum Posey, the team manager, first saw Leonard, he wasn't sure the young man was big enough to be a good first baseman. He told Leonard that they might have to hire another man to play first base. But when Posey saw Leonard play, he realized that Leonard was a good first baseman who also could hit. Posey turned out to be a great teacher, showing Leonard how to hold the bat, how to change the way he stood, and how to hit. He urged all the players to play hard but also to play a clean game.

The Grays were based in Homestead, Pennsylvania, a steel-mining town across the river from Pittsburgh. The team formed in 1910 when African American workers in the steel mills wanted to have something fun to do on the weekends. Their skills improved, and in 1932, they joined the Negro National League. At the time that Leonard was hired, Cum Posey was doing anything he could to get new players because he'd recently lost some good men to a rival team, the Pittsburgh Crawfords. Sometimes, Posey would steal players from other teams by asking them to talk to him on the Grays' bus. Before they could step off, the bus would drive away, with the new teammates still on board.

In Leonard's first year with the Grays, he made $125 a month and received an allowance of sixty cents a day for food. At that time, a person could buy bacon, eggs, and iced tea for just twenty-five cents, so he had more than enough to live on.

Leonard lived in Pittsburgh with some of his teammates. Since Pittsburgh was a much bigger city than Homestead, there was a lot to do. The players would go out at night and sometimes would stay out too late. Cum Posey didn't approve of their lifestyle, so he forced them to live in Homestead with the rest of the team.

Leonard didn't really like Homestead the first year that he lived there. He decided that he would finish the season with the Grays but would not go back the next year. In time, however, he grew to like Homestead and ended up playing for the Grays for the next seventeen years.

Playing the Game

The game of baseball was very different at the time of the Negro leagues. For one thing, games were much shorter than they are now; they lasted only about two hours. One way they were able to move things along was with solid pitching. Today, teams have relief pitchers, and three or four players might share pitching duties in one game. Negro league teams did not have that luxury; pitchers could throw well for all nine innings. A team would have three or four good pitchers, and if they couldn't last all nine innings of a game, they were not likely to stay on the team. Another reason the games were shorter was that the hitters did not wait to get signals from coaches. They would just step up to the plate and swing.

One of the things Buck Leonard did to improve his hitting was to watch the pitcher while he was warming up. He would watch the ball to see what kind of spin it had. When he came up to the plate, he would have a good idea of how to hit the pitch. He also worked hard on his fielding. He had a strong arm and he was good at handling both low throws and pop flies. Leonard played a little deeper at first base than did most first basemen. This helped him to make lots of plays that other first basemen might have missed.

Getting on a team in the Negro leagues wasn't easy. In order to keep their costs down, teams usually had only from fourteen to

Spectators watch the Homestead Grays play a baseball game at Forbes Field in Pittsburgh, Pennsylvania.

nineteen players. There was a lot of competition to get on teams, and just as much competition to stay on them. Because of that, players would often participate even if they were injured. They were afraid that if they didn't play, they would be replaced. Also, they did not get paid if they didn't play in a game. Buck Leonard often played through injuries. The only reason he wouldn't play was if he had a broken bone.

Negro league athletes often excelled at playing more than one position, or even coached in addition to playing their regular positions. Ted "Double Duty" Radcliffe often pitched one game of a doubleheader and then caught during the next. Unlike today, when professional baseball players often retire in their thirties, Negro league players often played for a long time. One of the most famous Negro league players was Cool Papa Bell. He retired when he was forty-three years old, and in his last year he hit .413. Buck Leonard didn't retire until he was forty-eight years old.

Spring Training

For most of the years Leonard played with the Homestead Grays, the team would start the year in Florida with a few weeks of spring training. The team played an exhibition game almost every day and did not have a lot of time to work on the basics of baseball. They might have five or six days of training and then would start playing local clubs and working their way north. The Grays and other teams also used spring training to scout out new players who might be good enough to join a Negro league team.

Spring training was always enjoyed by southern baseball fans. The Negro leagues had a lot of fans in the South but didn't play many games there during the regular season. Their fans had to follow the teams in African American newspapers.

The Regular Season

During the regular season, the Grays played a game almost every day; some days, they played more than one. They played each game as if it were the most important they'd ever played. In 1938, Wendell Smith, an African American reporter, wrote about the Grays, "They do not believe that any team can beat them. They don't give a hoot for umpires, fans, newspapermen, or anything else. Baseball is all they care about— it is their life."

Ted Radcliffe

Ted "Double Duty" Radcliffe

Ted "Double Duty" Radcliffe was one of the most interesting characters in the Negro leagues. Many people feel he has never gotten the attention he deserved. He was invited to play with the Illinois Giants when he was just sixteen years old, and he didn't retire until he was in his fifties. He got his nickname in 1932, when he played in a doubleheader in Yankee Stadium. In the first game, he played catcher for the great pitcher Satchel Paige, winning the game 5–0. Then, in the second game, Radcliffe pitched his team to a 4–0 win, earning the nickname Double Duty.

During the seventh inning of one game, Double Duty was injured. His manager wanted to take him out of the game but Double Duty told everyone that "they'd have to call the police" before he would let them take him out.

The first few years that Leonard was with the Grays, the team worked hard to get new players and improve their game. Leonard was a talented player and began to get a lot of recognition from the fans, from other players, and from newspapers. He was also a leader of the team and tried to set a good example on and off the field. By 1936, Leonard's third season with the Grays, the team finished second in the Negro National League. Leonard hit thirty-three home runs and batted .436.

It was in 1937 that the Grays really took off. In one game, they beat their rivals, the Pittsburgh Crawfords, 20–0. In that game, Leonard had three hits, including a grand slam. In an article that spring, a newspaper writer named Leonard the new superstar on the Grays. Leonard didn't pay much attention to what was written about him. He was just happy to play baseball.

One of the reasons the Grays did so well in 1937 was that Josh Gibson had joined the team. The manager of Gibson's old team owed money to Rufus "Sonnyman" Jackson, one of the owners of the Grays. To pay off his debt,

Gibson's manager was forced to let him join the Grays. Gibson added a lot to the team, and he was a great home-run hitter.

Leonard had a great year and was hitting .500 after the first half of the season, tying Gibson for the league lead in home runs. Leonard finished the year hitting .383, with 36 home runs. That year ended on another good note for Leonard. On December 31, he married Sarah Wroten. He had met her when he had worked at the funeral home in Rocky Mount. She had owned the funeral home but had sold it before she married Leonard. After they got married, Sarah taught first grade.

The next two years were even better for Leonard and the Grays. Many people say they were the best Grays team ever. In the first half of the 1938 season, the Grays won more than 80 percent of their games, and Leonard was hitting .480. At that point, he had gotten a base hit in every game but one. And he was starting to get even more attention for his fielding. In July, one newspaper reported that Leonard was

The Homestead Grays' first baseman, Buck Leonard, prepares to swing at a baseball during a Negro league game.

"without a doubt the best first baseman in Negro baseball." The Grays won the second half of the season and the Negro National League pennant.

The next year was no different. In one game against the Philadelphia Stars, Leonard hit two home runs, one of which was inside the park. (Leonard didn't hit many inside-the-park home runs during his career because he was not the fastest runner.) Both Josh Gibson and Leonard had great seasons, and newspapers began writing more stories about them. The newspaper writers thought that if the major leagues started to accept African Americans, Leonard and Gibson would be among the first players to join major league teams.

People who watched Negro league games and followed the men who played in the Negro leagues often thought of Leonard and Gibson together. They were sometimes called the Thunder Twins or the Dynamite Twins. They took turns batting third and fourth in the lineup, and pitchers were often worried about facing them. In 1938, Leonard, Gibson, and two of their other teammates acquired the nickname the Murderer's Row because they got so many hits. People often compared Leonard and Gibson to two famous white major league players from the New York Yankees. Leonard was compared to Lou Gehrig, and Gibson to Babe Ruth. Both were powerful hitting combinations, and the only difference between them as players was the color of their skin.

In 1940, the Thunder Twins were broken up when Gibson and a few other Grays went to play on a team in Mexico. Leonard had to work harder without Gibson on the team, but he lived up to the challenge. The Grays won the pennant again that year, and Leonard ended the season batting .376. The next year, the Grays won the Negro National League pennant by beating the New York Cubans in four out of five playoff games.

One of Leonard's favorite stories from his days in the Negro leagues took place sometime

Statistics

If you look at the sports page of any newspaper today, you can find the statistics of all the major league teams and players. You can find the number of home runs a player has hit or the number of runs he has batted in. In the early days of the Negro leagues, accurate statistics were not kept. Some of the games the teams played were not even reported. When the leagues did begin to keep statistics, a member of the team who was not playing in that game might keep the score. But not everyone knew how to score plays, and the score-keeping player might have to go into the game and turn the scoring over to another player.

In later years, some African American newspapers paid writers to travel with the teams and keep official scores. But this was not always much better than when the players kept score. The writer who traveled with the Grays often came late to the games and relied on the players to tell him what had happened so far. Thus, the Negro league records that we have now are not always accurate. The players didn't worry much about batting averages because they were too busy playing the game.

during the 1940 season. Leonard was sliding into second base when the throw came in from right field. The ball hit him in his armpit, but no one but Leonard knew that. So he ran all the way to home base with the ball tucked into his armpit. No one could figure out where the ball had gone. Once Leonard was safely at home base, he took the ball out of his armpit and threw it back onto the field. Of course, today this would be frowned upon, but this kind of crafty entertainment was applauded in the Negro leagues.

Another good story from Leonard's career is about the Newark, New Jersey, game where he hit his longest home run. People who were at that game say the ball went 400 to 500 feet. Double Duty Radcliffe said it "cleared the fence, the bleachers, a row of houses, and hit a big old water tower." People joked that the tower rained water for days from where it was hit by the ball.

Josh Gibson returned to the Grays in 1942, and the team won its sixth Negro National

League pennant. That year, the Grays played the Kansas City Monarchs of the Negro American League in the first Negro league World Series. The series was played in a different town each night. Unfortunately, the Grays lost all four games. That setback didn't keep them from continuing their winning ways, however. They won the Negro National League pennant again the next three years, for an amazing nine straight years of Negro National League championships.

The 1946 season did not begin well for the Homestead Grays. Cum Posey, the manager and owner of the team since 1911, died in March. The season ended badly as well. It was the first time in ten years that the Grays did not win the Negro National League pennant. The next year did not start well either. Josh Gibson died in January, and Leonard sorely missed the other half of the Thunder Twins. The Grays didn't get off to a good start and neither did Leonard. He missed the first three weeks of the season because of an injury, and then he missed other games during the season because of more injuries. Although

Josh Gibson is tagged out at home plate during the twelfth annual Negro league East-West All-Star Game on August 13, 1944.

Leonard ended up hitting .410 for the year, for the second year in a row the Grays did not win the Negro National League pennant.

The Grays—and Leonard—rebounded in 1948 and had one of their best seasons. They won the Negro National League pennant in an exciting playoff with the Baltimore Stars. Then they went on to win the Negro World Series by beating the Birmingham Black Barons four games to one. Leonard finished the year with a .391 average and was tied for the lead in home runs. At the end of the season, the fans honored him with a Buck Leonard Day at Griffith Stadium in Washington, D.C. They gave him an award, some clothes, and money that they collected for him at the front gate.

Team photo of the Homestead Grays in 1943. Buck Leonard is third from the right in the back row.

All-Star Games

One of the highlights of each season was the Negro leagues all-star game. It was usually played in Chicago in August and featured the best players from the Negro American League and the Negro National League. Participants were chosen by fans who voted for their favorite players. For many fans, the game was the high point of the year. In 1943, 51,723 people attended the game, proving what many people already knew: Baseball could attract a large crowd of African Americans. It showed owners of major league teams that African Americans would come to see other African Americans play, and it may be one of the reasons that integration of the major leagues eventually happened.

Buck Leonard played in his first all-star game in 1934. Except for two years when he was injured, he played in the next twelve all-star games. In most of those games, he was the starting first baseman. Each time he was selected to be on the team, he considered it a great honor. His first all-star game was memorable. He took his first plane trip to get to the game. It cost him forty-four of his own dollars to fly from Newark, New Jersey, to Chicago. In that game, he hit a sacrifice fly to tie the game in the tenth inning, and the Negro National League went on to win the exciting game in the eleventh inning.

In 1937, Leonard made the all-star team by winning the most votes of any Negro National League player. In the game, he got two hits, including a home run, to help his team win 7–2.

Winter Baseball

Baseball became a year-round game for many players who went south when cold weather ended the season in the North. Players had to find jobs during the winter months because Negro league baseball did not pay big salaries. What better thing to do than play baseball? Many players joined leagues in Mexico, Puerto

Rico, Cuba, the Dominican Republic, and
Venezuela. Winter baseball was a way for
players to continue to make money and play the
game they loved, but it was also a good way for
players to improve their skills. During the
regular season, there was no time for practice
because teams had to play a game every day.
They spent much of the rest of their time
traveling from place to place. But most winter
leagues played only a few games a week, so
there was enough time for players to work on
their hitting and fielding.

Like many other players in the Negro
leagues, Leonard had to play winter baseball to
make enough money to live on. His first season
playing winter baseball was in 1935. He played
in Puerto Rico and had a good season, hitting
.346. And with all the practice he was able to
do, his skills as a first baseman improved.
During that winter season, the Cincinnati Reds,
a white major league team, came to Puerto Rico
for spring training. They played Leonard's team
several times, and although they were a worthy

opponent, Leonard's team beat them two out of three games.

The next winter, Leonard went to Cuba to play winter baseball. He had another solid season, and his team won the pennant by just one game. That winter, Leonard was thrown out of one game for arguing with an umpire. Even though the umpire didn't speak English, he knew that what Leonard had to say wasn't good. He ejected Leonard, who had to pay ten dollars to play the next day. That was the first of only two times that Leonard was ever thrown out of a game.

Leonard went to Cuba again the next winter with an all-star team that included many members of the Grays. They traveled from Miami to Cuba by boat and played all around Cuba. Leonard continued to play winter baseball in Cuba and in Puerto Rico for the next few years. During World War II, he was not able to play winter baseball because he had to take a job to help the war effort. He worked at the railroad station in his hometown unloading

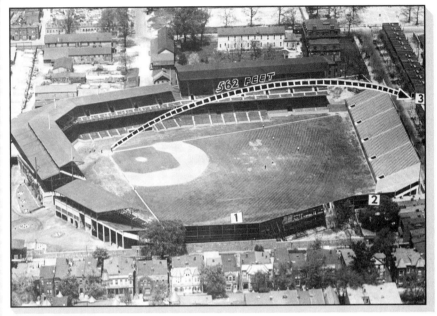

This is an aerial view of Griffith Stadium, where the Homestead Grays played their home games.

boxcars. It was hard work and it hurt his back, but he was glad to be able to spend time at home. After the war, Leonard was able to return to playing baseball in the off-season. He played in Venezuela in 1945 with an American all-star team. On his team was Jackie Robinson, the player who would soon be the first African American to join a white major league team.

The Negro Leagues: Life on the Road

Today, baseball players make millions of dollars a year, travel by plane, and stay in comfortable hotels while they're on the road. Things were very different when Buck Leonard was playing baseball in the Negro leagues.

A Game Every Day

The regular baseball season lasted from May 1 to September 15, and during that time many Negro league teams would play about 200 games. Sometimes, a team would play three games in one day, each game in a different town. They might play a game at ten in the morning, start another at three in the afternoon, and begin the last at half past six that night. Sometimes, the last game would get cut short if it became too dark to continue. Right after the last out, the team would get onto the bus and would begin the trip to the next game. They would eat on the way or maybe take a nap. It was a difficult schedule. A team might travel 30,000 to 40,000 miles in one season.

Negro league games usually took place on Tuesday and Thursday evenings, and on Saturdays and Sundays. These were the times when most people were not working and could visit the ballpark. In order to earn enough money, Negro league teams had to play a game on other days, too. So on Monday, Wednesday, and Friday, they often held exhibition games against local teams. Traveling around to these games against local teams was called barnstorming.

Travel by Bus

To play a game every day, teams had to do a lot of traveling. In Leonard's early years in baseball, his teams traveled by car. Each team usually had two cars, and six or seven players had to jam into each one. A few years after Leonard joined the Grays, the team acquired a bus.

The Grays spent a lot of time on their bus, and one way to pass the time was to gamble on games of dice or cards. Unlike some of the other players, Leonard didn't gamble, and he often spent time on the bus doing crossword puzzles. Another way to make time go faster was to sing. Leonard and his teammates would sing late at night and would continue until they fell asleep.

If the Grays lost a game, they would often talk about it on the bus that night. They would figure out what they could have done better and wouldn't go to sleep until they knew what they were going to do the next day to improve.

Travel by bus wasn't easy. Double Duty Radcliffe remembered a time when he was driving his team's bus in Georgia. They stopped at a gas station whose owner wouldn't let them use the hose to get gas, telling them it was for

Buck Leonard *(right)* shares a laugh with Dave Barnhill during a winter baseball game in Cuba in 1948.

whites only. The owner told them if they wanted to buy gas they would have to put the gas in a Coke bottle and fill their tank that way. Double Duty decided to leave without buying any gas. A few miles later, the bus ran out of gas and the team had to push the bus ten miles to get to the next station. But the men made pushing the bus fun and were proud that Radcliffe had refused to buy gas at that station.

During World War II, when many resources were rationed (restricted), teams were allowed to use only a certain amount of gas each month. They could go only 700 miles per month, and when their gas ran out they would have to take the train. In Leonard's seventeen years with the Grays, they missed only two games. Once, the Grays' bus broke down in Maryland on the way to a game in Washington, D.C. That didn't stop them from getting to the game, though. They called three taxis and made it to the game in time.

Hotels and Restaurants

Many places where the Grays played didn't have hotels where African Americans were allowed to stay. In those towns and cities, the team would stay at a YMCA or at a rooming house. Sometimes they would even have to sleep on the bus. Although some towns they stayed in did have African American hotels, those weren't always nice places to stay. One hotel Leonard and his teammates often stayed in when they were in New Orleans had so many bedbugs that the players had to spread layers of newspapers over the beds before they could lie down. They also made sure to sleep with the lights on to help keep away the bugs.

Getting food was sometimes difficult, too. Since many restaurants refused to serve African Americans, teams had to find food where they could and often brought their own food on the bus. Sometimes, there would be a player on the team who looked white. He would go into a whites-only restaurant and buy food for the other players. Sometimes, teams had players from Cuba or Puerto Rico who were allowed into white restaurants. Even though they looked like African Americans, if they spoke with an accent, whites would allow them into the restaurant.

Ballparks

There were few African American ballparks when Leonard was playing baseball. The Grays

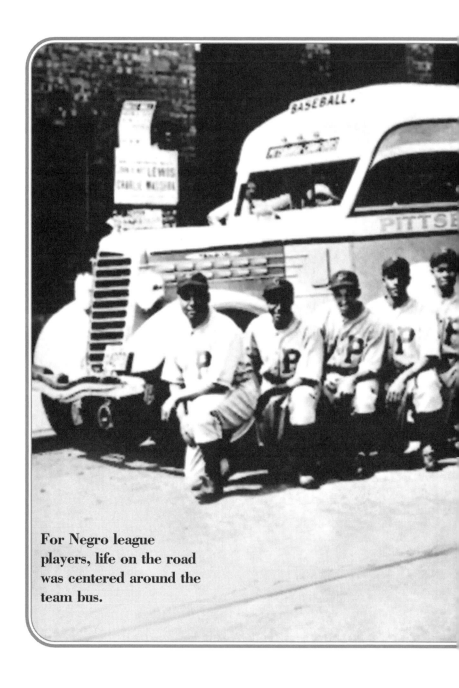

For Negro league
players, life on the road
was centered around the
team bus.

never had their own ballpark and had to use parks of other Negro league teams, or of major league teams. The Pittsburgh Crawfords, another area Negro league team, had their own park built by their owner, Gus Greenlee. Greenlee Field was also the Grays' home park for several years. The Grays played there when the Crawfords were out of town. Greenlee Field was never in very good shape. There was no roof over the stands and no clubhouse for the players to change into their uniforms.

When Greenlee Field was torn down after the 1938 season, the Grays used Forbes Field, the ballpark of the Pittsburgh Pirates. The Grays also sometimes used Griffith Stadium in Washington, D.C., as their home ballpark. In Washington, the Grays would often play for a large crowd. This was especially true during World War II, when people couldn't travel far. People had to find entertainment close to home. The largest crowd Buck Leonard remembered playing for was 30,000 at Griffith Stadium in 1942.

Negro League Fans

African American spectators watch a Negro league baseball game at Forbes Field in Pittsburgh, Pennsylvania.

For many fans, a baseball game was something to look forward to all week. People worked hard at their jobs and at home, but on a day when they were going to a baseball game, life might have seemed a little easier. Going to a game could make people forget about all the work they had to do. Games were also a place to see friends and neighbors and to talk about favorite players. It wasn't just the games that were entertaining. There were also activities before the game, such as races between the fastest players on each team or wrestling matches between the team mascots. Sometimes, the players would do a little act between innings or during the game. Lloyd "Pepper" Bassett, a catcher for the Pittsburgh Crawfords, would catch part of the game sitting in a rocking chair. It was always an exciting day when a Negro league team came to town.

Segregation often made life on the road difficult for Negro league players, particularly in southern towns.

There was a drawback to playing in Washington, D.C.: It was 290 miles away from Pittsburgh, so on days when the Grays had a game there, they would have to leave Pittsburgh at four in the morning and wouldn't arrive until noon. They would play one game, or sometimes a doubleheader, and then get back on the bus at nine at night. The bus would arrive back in Pittsburgh at five the next morning. That night they might play a game against a local team.

Leonard preferred it when the Grays played at Forbes Field. During the years when he lived in Pittsburgh, he could take the trolley to the ballpark. When he lived in Homestead, it was a short bus ride to the ballpark. He could sleep in, go to breakfast with his teammates, and then take the bus to the field.

Salaries

Players in the Negro leagues never made much money. Teams had to depend on what they could make from admissions to each game.

Greenlee Field, home to the Pittsburgh Crawfords, was the only stadium owned by a Negro league team.

They might make a lot on a weekend when many people could come to a game or when they played in a big ballpark. Teams called those days when they could make a lot of money "getting out of the hole" days. Other days, playing exhibition games in smaller towns, they might not make as much. Many players were paid a share of what the team made for each game, so if the team did not make a lot, the players didn't make a lot either.

Negro league players made much less than white major league players. In Buck Leonard's highest-paid year, he made $4,500 for the regular season. More than ten years earlier, Babe Ruth, the famous major league ballplayer had made $80,000 per year. But African American baseball players were often making much more than other African Americans who weren't playing baseball. Many former players say they were glad to be making a regular salary doing something they loved. They also got respect and public recognition. And they got to travel and see places they might never have seen otherwise.

Gus Greenlee, owner of the Pittsburgh Crawfords

When Leonard was first playing baseball, he did not earn a regular salary but instead was paid a share of each game. In the late 1930s, he was earning about $125 a month. But that was only for the four and a half months of the baseball season, so he had to play winter baseball also. At that time, his wife was earning about $48 a month teaching first grade. Without her salary, Leonard would have had to give up baseball. Later, as the Grays began to earn more money and as Leonard improved as a player, he earned a regular salary. During World War II, the Grays made a lot of money because so many people went to see baseball games. By 1943, the Grays were one of the highest-paid teams in Negro league baseball, and Buck Leonard and Josh Gibson were earning about two times as much as other players on the team. That year Leonard was offered $1,000 a month to play baseball in Mexico, but he stayed with the Grays when they matched the offer, in addition to agreeing to pay for his expenses at home and on the road. Leonard made his highest salary in 1944, when he earned $4,500 plus his food and a place to stay on the road and at home. This was only for the regular season, but with winter baseball he could make as much as $10,000 a year.

Leonard and the other players had to use part of their salary to buy their own equipment. They had to buy their gloves, shoes, sweatshirts, and socks. They got one home uniform and one road uniform at the beginning of the season, but they were not allowed to keep them at the end of the season. Umpires did not get equipment either. Mo Harris, an umpire who worked in the Negro leagues, used to sell his equipment to a pawnshop at the end of a season. At the beginning of the next season, he would show up at the first game and tell the team that he needed to be paid so he could buy back his equipment. He would get his money and then go to the pawnshop to get his mask, shin guards, and chest protector so they could start the game.

Integration and the End of the Negro Leagues

Many Negro leaguers knew they were good enough to play in the major leagues. Buck Leonard believed that "regardless of what color you were, if you could play baseball, you ought to be allowed to play anywhere that you could play." He and his teammates thought that someday African Americans would be allowed to join major league teams. Sometimes, newspaper writers would ask the players what they thought could be done to speed things up so that African Americans could play on major league teams. The players didn't think that holding demonstrations or signing petitions would do any good. They told the writers that they were

Jackie Robinson, in military uniform, signs a minor league contract
with the Brooklyn Dodgers in 1945.

welcome to do that kind of thing. The players wanted to concentrate on playing baseball.

Even though the Negro league players looked forward to the day when they would be allowed to play in the major leagues, they worried that if major league owners were forced to hire African Americans, the owners would make it hard on the players. In addition, African American owners of Negro league teams knew that integration would hurt their own teams. When the major leagues hired away the Negro league's star players, the quality of play on Negro league teams would drop, and the fans might stop coming to their games.

In 1938, Buck Leonard thought he might have a chance to join the major leagues. After playing a doubleheader in Washington, D.C., he and Josh Gibson were invited to meet with Clark Griffith, the owner of the Washington Senators. Griffith asked Leonard and Gibson if they would like to play in the majors. Of course, they told him they wanted to. But Griffith said that no team in the major leagues was ready to hire African American players. It wasn't until seven years later, in 1945, that the first steps would be taken toward integration.

That year, two major league teams allowed select African American players to come to spring tryouts. The Boston Red Sox invited Jackie Robinson, Sam Jethroe, and Marvin Williams to attend a tryout, but none was asked to join the team. The Brooklyn Dodgers allowed two players to try out that same year. Those same players were not invited to join the Dodgers either. But Branch Rickey, the owner of the Dodgers, knew that an African American player would soon join the major leagues.

Branch Rickey had been thinking about integration for a long time. He thought that segregation was wrong, and he was interested in doing what he could to bring change to baseball. He was also interested in making the Dodgers a better team. So, in 1945, he began sending scouts around the country to check out African American players. He and his scouts were looking for players who were young, since they would probably have to play in the minor leagues for a few years before joining a major league team. He also wanted players who would be able to handle the pressure that the first African American player in the major leagues would most likely feel. Jackie Robinson was the man the scouts found.

Jackie Robinson was not recognized as the best player in the Negro leagues. But he was smart, and he was willing to stand up to people who didn't think African Americans should join the major leagues. When Jackie Robinson was in the army, he had refused to go to the back of the bus when the driver ordered him to. He was taken to court, but the charges against him were eventually dropped. Also, as a college athlete at the University of California at Los Angeles (UCLA), he had interacted with white teammates and opponents; he was no stranger to the prejudice he would encounter.

Near the end of the 1945 baseball season, Jackie Robinson met with Branch Rickey. Robinson was invited to join the Dodgers' minor league team, the Montreal Royals. He accepted,

Cover of the first issue of *Colored Baseball & Sports Monthly*

African American Baseball Writers

For many fans of Negro league baseball, African American newspapers were a way to keep up with their favorite teams. The newspapers came out once a week and had a large base of readers. In the days before television, newspapers were a way for people to catch up on the news. The newspapers didn't have big budgets, so the men who wrote about sports often had to write stories for other parts of the paper as well.

The reporters had to deal with many of the same problems that the players faced. They had to cover as many as three games each day and spent much of their time traveling between games. They faced the same prejudice as the players and weren't allowed to eat in certain restaurants or to stay in white hotels. The writers called attention to these problems and often wrote stories about how African Americans should be accepted into the major leagues. One writer wrote, "The ban against Negro players in the major leagues is a silly one, and one that should be removed." The stories that these reporters wrote may have helped to speed up integration.

and the following spring he reported for training in Florida. Getting to training camp showed Robinson that things might not be easy for him. On his way to Florida, he and his wife were forced to get off the plane and their seats were given to two white people. They had trouble finding a place to stay, and when they tried to take a bus, they were forced to sit in the back.

Although many people were happy that an African American player was taking the first steps to integrating the major leagues, others still believed that African Americans were not equal and should not be allowed to play on the same teams as white players. People in one of the towns where the Dodgers were scheduled to train even prohibited the team from playing there because they had an African American player. Some major league players were so unhappy about Robinson joining the Dodgers that they threatened to go on strike if they had to play against him. When Robinson started playing, though, his courage and superior skills won most people over, and players and fans quickly accepted him.

Jackie Robinson was not the only player from the Negro leagues at the Dodgers' spring training camp that year. Johnny Wright, one of Buck Leonard's teammates from the Homestead Grays, had been invited to join the team. He did not handle the pressure as well as Jackie Robinson did, and he returned to the Grays after just one season.

Two other Negro league players were also hired to play for the Dodgers later that spring. Roy Campanella and Don Newcombe were sent to play for the Dodgers in Nashua, New Hampshire, and later played in Montreal with Robinson. By 1949, all three men were playing for the Brooklyn Dodgers.

For Buck Leonard and some of the other Negro league stars, integration came too late. Leonard was almost forty years old when Jackie Robinson began playing with the Dodgers. Major league teams were looking for players who were young and who would be able to play for the team for at least four or five years. Leonard knew he wouldn't be able to play well for that long. He also worried about the pressure that an African American would face in the major leagues.

Breakup of the Negro Leagues

After Jackie Robinson joined the Brooklyn Dodgers, many of the problems that Negro league team owners and players had anticipated became reality. As more and more African Americans joined the major leagues, the Negro league teams were left with fewer good players. None of the teams that lost players to the major leagues were paid for the players who had left. And fans had begun going to major league games to see their favorite African American players. Without fans paying to see the games, Negro league teams could not afford to pay their players as much.

Negro league teams began to break up in 1948. The Negro National League broke up that same year. Some of the teams that were left in the league joined teams in the Negro American League, but by 1953 there were only four teams left. A few teams continued to play until 1960.

Last Years with the Grays

At the beginning of the 1949 season, the Grays joined the Negro American League. The Negro National League had broken up the year before, but the Grays were determined to keep playing. They soon found that they did not have the kind of team they were used to. Nine of their players had joined major league teams. The Grays were able to rebuild their team, but it was never as good. They decided to leave the Negro American League and to finish the season playing games in the South. The other teams in the league were not very good, so the Grays ended the first half of the season with a 24–2 record.

After the 1949 season was over, Leonard joined the New York Stars. The team was made up of players from many of the remaining Negro league teams. The Stars

**Baseball fans in Montreal seek Jackie Robinson's autograph before
an exhibition game in April 1947.**

played some games around New York State, and when the weather turned too cold for baseball, the team moved south. The Stars stopped along the way to play wherever they could. They played games in cow pastures, ball fields, and prison yards—whatever it took to get a game together every day. When the weather became too cold in the South, the team traveled to Venezuela. They played there for about two months, and then Leonard returned home to Rocky Mount and prepared for his last season with the Grays.

The 1950 Grays team was not much better than the one the year before. Once again, they played in a southern league. There was not a lot of money for salaries or travel, and few people came to see the team play. The Grays asked Leonard to be the business manager, but he didn't want to handle the money or be a manager. At the end of the season, the team got together and decided they didn't want to play anymore. After seventeen years with the Grays, Leonard had to decide what to do next.

Playing in Mexico

Buck Leonard was not ready to quit baseball, so he decided to play for a team in Mexico. He had been invited to play for the St. Louis Browns, a major league team, but he knew he was too old. He was forty-five, and his legs weren't strong enough to play every day. Since teams in the Mexican leagues played only three games a week, there was plenty of time for him to rest between games.

Each week, the Mexican league teams played Thursday night, Saturday night, and Sunday morning in Mexico City. Leonard and his teammates had a lot of time to do other things between games. Some days they would sit in plazas and watch people. Other days they would go to bullfights and rooster fights. The bullfights were the high point of the week in Mexico City. They took place on Saturday afternoons, and 50,000 people would attend. The bulls and bullfighters were from Spain and always put on an exciting show.

Though he was still a good player when baseball was integrated, Buck Leonard, at forty years old, realized he was too old to make it to the major leagues.

The first three summers Leonard lived in Mexico, he played on a team in the main Mexican league. They were based in a town called Torreón, and they were called the Peas. Leonard and another player nicknamed themselves the "black-eyed peas." Leonard continued to hit well and was a better hitter than most of the other players. He had averages of .322, .325, and .332 the first three years. Leonard also played in Mexico during the winter season. He would go home to Rocky Mount for a few weeks after the summer season and would then return to Mexico. The first winter he played for a team in Obregón. The next two winters he played in Xalapa (now called Jalapa) for the Hot Peppers. In 1953, Leonard was voted the most valuable player for the Hot Peppers. At the end of the 1953 season, he returned to Rocky Mount and was asked to play for a team in Portsmouth, Virginia. They were a Class B major league team and needed someone to help them win the pennant. Leonard took the place of their regular first baseman and hit .333 while he was there.

When Leonard returned to Mexico for the summer season in 1954, he played for Durango, a team in the Mexican Central League. This league was not as good as the league in which he had played during his first few years in Mexico. He played for them again in 1955, but he did not play winter baseball either year. Instead, he stayed in Rocky Mount and worked at a garage. At the end of the summer season in 1955, Leonard decided to quit playing baseball. He was forty-eight years old and had arthritis. His back hurt, and he was tired after a lifetime of playing baseball almost year-round. He knew he could not play another year. It was time to find a different kind of work.

Life After Baseball

Buck Leonard returned to Rocky Mount in 1955 to live full-time. He got a job with the Watson Company, delivering cigars to stores. A few years later, he took a job with the Rocky Mount school system as a truant officer. Every day, Leonard went to two schools to pick up a list of students who had not shown up that day and would visit their houses to find out why they were not in school. Sometimes he would find that the children did not have sufficient clothes or shoes, and he would try to help out the families. Leonard worked as a truant officer for ten years before teaching physical education in the Rocky Mount school system for another two years.

In 1966, Leonard's wife, Sarah, died. Sarah's death was very hard on him. They had never had children, and Leonard was left alone. It was the worst time in his life. To make matters worse, his mother died two years later.

While Leonard worked for the school system, he also earned a license to sell real estate. Eventually, he worked part-time selling real estate while he continued to work for the schools. In 1970, when Leonard was sixty-two, he retired from the school system but continued selling real estate full-time until 1986. He also kept busy by working as the vice president of the Rocky Mount baseball team, a Class A farm team for the Cincinnati Reds, the Detroit Tigers, and the Philadelphia Phillies.

Retirement

Even after he stopped working full-time, Leonard stayed very active. In addition to selling real estate, he taught a Sunday school class at the St. James Baptist Church in Rocky Mount, the church he had attended for more than seventy years. He raised beagle hounds, hunted rabbits and squirrels, and went deep-sea fishing. But in 1986, he had a stroke that paralyzed his right side. He worked hard to regain the use of his right hand and to get around, but the stroke slowed him down. He had to stop going to church and had to settle for watching baseball on television instead of going to games. A few months after suffering the stroke, he married a woman named Lugenia Fox. The marriage kept up his spirits.

Awards and Recognition

For many years after Leonard retired from baseball, there was little interest in the Negro leagues or their players. But in 1970, the great pitcher Satchel Paige became the first Negro league player to be honored by the Baseball Hall of Fame. Finally, interest in the Negro leagues began to pick up. All of a sudden, there were books and movies and television shows about the Negro leagues. The players began to have reunions and go to special events.

Buck Leonard enjoys his induction into the Baseball Hall of Fame in 1972.

Leonard and other players were glad the Negro leagues were finally being recognized. It was important for people to remember what the Negro leagues had been like and what they had meant to the fans who had gone to their games. Because there were few official records of what things were like in the Negro leagues, it was up to the players to tell their stories for future generations. In July 2000, the Baseball Hall of Fame received $250,000 to study the history of African Americans in baseball. It is hoped that this project will also help tell the story of the Negro leagues.

The Negro Baseball Hall of History first opened in 1982 in Ashland, Kentucky. People hoped that this would be a way for the Negro leagues to at last be recognized and remembered. But the museum didn't last. Although some players sent photos or clippings from newspapers about the leagues, there weren't enough donated items to fill the museum. Players hadn't been allowed to keep their uniforms at the end of each season. Bats and balls belonged to the team.

Also, since Ashland, Kentucky, was not close to a major city, it did not attract a lot of visitors.

Another museum to honor the Negro leagues opened in 1991: The Negro Leagues Baseball Museum, located in Kansas City, Missouri. The museum has many exhibits and sometimes hosts reunions of Negro league players.

After retirement, Buck Leonard was often honored at local events called hot stove leagues. These events would take place in the winter to get people excited for the upcoming season. They would gather to talk about how they thought their favorite teams would do once the season started. Leonard was invited to attend many of these events, where he would talk about his experiences in baseball and share his thoughts on teams and players. Leonard's home town of Rocky Mount honored him by naming the local Little League baseball field Buck Leonard Park. He was also inducted into the North Carolina Sports Hall of Fame in 1974.

Leonard received national recognition at major league events. Some major league teams

A ninety-year-old Buck Leonard reflects on his baseball career in his hometown of Rocky Mount, North Carolina, on September 4, 1997.

have special nights to honor Negro league players, and Leonard was often invited to attend. He went to the 1993 All-Star Game in Baltimore, and he was the honorary captain of the National League team at the 1994 All-Star Game in Pittsburgh. Leonard was glad for all of this recognition, but his proudest moment was when he was inducted into the Baseball Hall of Fame.

Hall of Fame

Leonard had many exciting moments in his baseball career, but he said, "[The] biggest thrill I ever got was when I went into the Hall of Fame . . . [It] was something that I dreamed of. That is the high point of baseball. I had no idea that would ever happen to me."

Leonard may have been right to think that he would never be in the Baseball Hall of Fame. From the time that the Hall of Fame began in 1936 until 1971, when Satchel Paige was finally elected, no players from the Negro leagues were in the Hall of Fame. In 1971, a special group

This building on 18th Street and Vine Street in Kansas City, Missouri, hosts the Negro Leagues Baseball Museum and the American Jazz Museum.

was formed to choose Negro leaguers to be added to the Hall of Fame, and they selected nine players between 1971 and 1977. Buck Leonard and Josh Gibson were inducted in 1972. Many Negro leaguers followed, and by 2000 there were seventeen included in the Hall of Fame.

When Satchel Paige was inducted into the Hall of Fame in 1971, Buck Leonard was very excited. He had never expected to see a Negro league player accepted, and although he had visited the Hall of Fame before, he had never felt that he had a special reason to be there. Paige's inclusion made Leonard feel that he was part of the Hall at last. He would feel an even greater sense of belonging the following year when he joined Paige in the Hall of Fame.

Monte Irvin, another former Negro leaguer and friend of Leonard's, worked in the baseball commissioner's office in New York City. In early 1972, Irvin invited Leonard to help pick a Negro league all-star team to be engraved on a plaque for the Hall of Fame. Leonard agreed

Buck Leonard accepts his plaque from baseball commissioner
Bowie Kuhn as Leonard is inducted into the Baseball Hall of Fame.

to make the trip, expecting to see some old friends and discuss the players to be included. When he arrived, he was surprised to see the commissioner of baseball, reporters, and other important people there. He was told that Josh Gibson had been selected to join the Hall of Fame, and Leonard agreed to answer some questions about his old friend. Up on the platform, Leonard was stunned to learn that he, too, had been selected to join the Hall of Fame. He thanked everyone for honoring him, and because he could not think of anything else to say, he invited people to ask him questions. Afterward, Leonard said that he hoped he would not wake up and realize it had been a dream. It was the greatest moment of his life.

The official ceremony to induct Buck Leonard into the Hall of Fame took place on August 7, 1972, in Cooperstown, New York. In his speech, Leonard talked about how he and the other Negro leaguers had contributed to the game of baseball. They had played with bats and balls

Sculpture of Satchel Paige in the Baseball Hall of Fame

Negro Leaguers in the Baseball Hall of Fame

Players	Year Inducted	Position
Satchel Paige	1971	Pitcher
Buck Leonard	1972	First Base
Josh Gibson	1972	Catcher
Monte Irvin	1973	Outfield
Cool Papa Bell	1974	Outfield
Judy Johnson	1975	Third Base
Oscar Charleston	1976	First Base/Outfield
Martin Dihigo	1977	Pitcher/Outfield
Pop Lloyd	1977	Shortstop
Rube Foster	1981	Pitcher/Manager
Ray Dandridge	1987	Third Base
Leon Day	1995	Pitcher/Outfield/Second Base
Willie Foster	1996	Pitcher
Willie Wells	1997	Shortstop
Wilber "Bullet" Rogan	1998	Pitcher
Joe Williams	1999	Pitcher
Turkey Stearnes	2000	Outfield

JOSHUA (JOSH) GIBSON
NEGRO LEAGUES 1930-1946
CONSIDERED GREATEST SLUGGER IN NEGRO
BASEBALL LEAGUES. POWER-HITTING CATCHER
WHO HIT ALMOST 800 HOME RUNS IN LEAGUE
AND INDEPENDENT BASEBALL DURING HIS
17-YEAR CAREER. CREDITED WITH HAVING
BEEN NEGRO NATIONAL LEAGUE BATTING
CHAMPION IN 1936-38-42-45.

WALTER FENNER LEONARD
"BUCK"
NEGRO LEAGUES 1933-1950
FIRST BASEMAN OF HOMESTEAD GRAYS WHEN
TEAM WON NEGRO NATIONAL LEAGUE PENNANT
NINE YEARS IN A ROW, 1937-1945. TEAMED
WITH JOSH GIBSON TO FORM MOST FEARED
BATTING TWOSOME IN NEGRO BASEBALL FROM
1937 TO 1946. RANKED AMONG NEGRO HOME
RUN LEADERS. WON NEGRO NATIONAL LEAGUE
BATTING TITLE WITH 391 AVERAGE IN 1948.

WILLIAM HARRIDGE
PRESIDENT OF AMERICAN LEAGUE 1931-1958
AFTER SERVING AS SECRETARY OF
LEAGUE 1927-1931 AND SECRETARY TO
A.L. PRESIDENT 1911-1927.
CHAIRMAN OF AMERICAN LEAGUE
BOARD OF DIRECTORS 1958-1971.

ROSS MIDDLEBROOK YOUNGS
"PEP"
NEW YORK N.L. 1917-1926
STAR RIGHT FIELDER OF CHAMPION GIANTS
OF 1921-22-23-24 WHEN HE BATTED .327, .331,
.336, AND .356 COMPILED LIFETIME AVERAGE
OF .322. TOPPING .300 IN NINE OF TEN YEARS.
TWICE MADE 200 OR MORE HITS IN A SEASON.
LED LEAGUE IN DOUBLES IN 1919 AND RUNS
SCORED IN 1923 LED N.L. OUTFIELDERS
IN ASSISTS TWICE AND TIED ONCE.

Hall of Fame plaques celebrating the careers of Josh Gibson, Buck Leonard, William Harridge, and Ross Youngs

just like the major league players of the time. Many of them knew they were good enough to have played in the major leagues if they had been allowed to. But the most important thing was that they had loved the game and had had a great time playing it.

Buck Leonard died of a stroke on November 27, 1997. In his autobiography, *Buck Leonard: The Black Lou Gehrig,* he wrote, "I would like to be remembered as playing the game, and playing it clean and hard. And for having the respect of the fans." Judging from the legacy Buck Leonard left behind, it appears that he has received his wish.

Timeline

September 8, 1907 Walter Fenner "Buck" Leonard is born in Rocky Mount, North Carolina.

1913 Starts school.

1919–1921 Works in factory after school.

1921 Finishes school.

1921–1932 Works for Atlantic Coastline Railroad Shop.

1921–1933 Plays for Rocky Mount Elks and Rocky Mount Black Swans.

1933 Plays for Dougherty's Black Revels in Portsmouth, North Carolina.

1933 Plays for Baltimore Stars.

1933–1934 Plays for the Brooklyn Royal Giants.

1934–1950 Plays for the Homestead Grays (Negro leagues).

1937 Wins Negro National League batting championship.

December 31, 1937 Marries Sarah
Wroten.

1938 Wins Negro National League
batting championship.

1948 Wins Negro National League
batting championship.

1951–1953 Plays for Torreón
(Mexican league).

1954–1955 Plays for Durango
(Mexican league).

1955 Retires from baseball.

1958–1968 Works as truant officer for
Rocky Mount schools.

1968–1970 Works as physical
education teacher for Rocky Mount
schools.

August 7, 1972 Inducted into Baseball
Hall of Fame.

1986 Marries Lugenia Fox.

November 27, 1997 Dies in Rocky
Mount, North Carolina.

Glossary

barnstorming Traveling around the country playing exhibition games against local teams.

clubhouse A room at a ballpark where players can change into their uniforms and prepare for games.

doubleheader Two games played against the same team in one day.

exhibition A public showing of skills.

farm team A minor league team that is linked to a particular major league team.

grand slam A home run with the bases loaded that scores four runs.

induct To formally accept into a group, usually with a ceremony.

inside-the-park home run A hit that allows the batter to score even though the ball does not leave the field of play.

integration The bringing together of different races, groups, or classes.

league A group of teams that play games mostly against other teams in the group.

pennant The division or league championship.

petition A document signed by many people to show support for a cause.

prejudice Irrationally disliking someone because of his or her race, group, or religion.

rooming house A house where people can rent rooms.

sacrifice fly A fly ball that allows a runner to advance or score after it is caught by a fielder.

segregation The separation of one race, group, or class from another.

semiprofessional Playing a sport for pay but not as a full-time occupation.

Supreme Court The highest court in the United States.

union (labor union) A group of workers who join together for better wages and working conditions.

For More Information

National Baseball Hall of Fame and Museum
and National Baseball Hall of Fame Library
25 Main Street
P.O. Box 590
Cooperstown, NY 13326
(888) HALL-OF-FAME (425-5633)
Web site: http://baseballhalloffame.org

Negro Leagues Baseball Museum
1616 E. 18th Street
Kansas City, MO 64108-1610
(816) 221-1920
e-mail: nlmuseum@hotmail.com
Web site: http://www.nlbm.com

Web Sites

The Baseball Online Library
http://web2.sportsline.com/u/baseball/bol/sabr/
    tbi/index.html

Black Baseball's Negro Baseball Leagues
http://www.blackbaseball.com

Major League Baseball
http://www.mlb.com

Negro League Baseball
http://www.negroleaguebaseball.com

For Further Reading

Brashler, William. *The Story of Negro League Baseball.* New York: Ticknor & Fields, 1994.

Chadwick, Bruce. *When the Game Was Black and White: The Illustrated History of the Negro Leagues.* New York: Abbeville Press, 1992.

Fremon, David K. *The Negro Baseball Leagues.* New York: New Discovery Books, 1994.

Leonard, Buck, and James A. Riley. *Buck Leonard: The Black Lou Gehrig: The Hall of Famer's Story in His Own Words.* New York: Carroll & Graf Publishers, Inc., 1995.

McKissack, Patricia C., and Fredrick McKissack Jr. *Black Diamond: The Story of the Negro Baseball Leagues.* New York: Scholastic, 1994.

Riley, James A. *The Negro Leagues* (African-American Achievers). New York: Chelsea House, 1996.

Winter, Jonah. *Fair Ball! 14 Great Stars from Baseball's Negro Leagues.* New York: Scholastic, 1999.

Index

About the Author

Simone Payment has a degree in psychology from Cornell University and a master's degree in elementary education from Wheelock College. She has taught elementary school, has worked in book publishing, and currently works for a health care company. She is a long-suffering Boston Red Sox fan.

Acknowledgments

The author would like to thank Howard Cooper, Lori Cooper, Marina Lang, Jennifer Marcus, and Joseph Wyman for their suggestions and support.

Photo Credits

Cover, pp. 11, 39, 55, 83 © Baseball Hall of Fame Museum; pp. 4, 7, 12 © Library of Congress; pp. 8, 28, 36, 61 © Hulton Archive; pp. 15, 16, 20, 33, 45, 51, 62, 64, 66, 70, 80, 100 © Corbis; pp. 25, 74 © Schomberg Collection, New York Public Library; p. 46 © Carnegie Library of Pittsburgh, Pennsylvania; pp. 58–59, 89, 92, 94, 96, 98 © Associated Press.

Series Design and Layout

Claudia Carlson